PLAYING IT THEIR WAY

Karen Z. Kowalski

m b b

MOUSEBOX BOOKS
www.mouseboxbooks.com

First edition.
10-digit ISBN: 0-9786735-0-6
13-digit ISBN: 978-0-9786735-0-5

Library of Congress data pending

Edited by Patti Verbanas
Cover & interior design by Conker Tree Design, www.conkertree.com
Cover illustration by Leeza Hernandez
Photography by Ed Pagliarini
Stock photography: Absolutvision.com, Photodisc, Conker Tree Design

For Bam.

Contents

Introduction

Find Your Own "Summer A."

I t is only fitting that I begin with the story of "Summer A.," because you would not be reading this book had she not come into my life. My work with Summer began when she was 15 and her mother called to inquire about piano lessons. Most teachers would have no difficulty with this request. However, there was something very special about Summer: She had developmental delays, Tourette's Syndrome and Attention Deficit Disorder. Mrs. A. explained that Summer's music teacher at school told her not to bother with music lessons since, she said, "Summer cannot learn music." Fortunately, Mrs. A. did not believe this teacher and asked if I would meet with her and assess her ability to learn. At the time I was studying for my degree in Occupational Therapy and was up for the challenge, so I agreed to take her on as a student.

A decade later, Summer is still taking piano lessons, has participated in numerous concerts and along the way has become a friend. And, since we learned this process together, I consider Summer one of my greatest teachers. It wasn't an easy road, however. At first, I floundered, trying to teach her using standard music books and basic adaptations. As her lessons progressed, I realized that I was on my own and had to create a teaching method that was tailored to her abilities. My goal was to make the lessons fun for Summer and to maintain her enthusiasm for learning.

Success stories, like Summer's experience, are a testament that students with special needs *can* learn music. They just need a teacher—like you—to show them how. Throughout this book, I will ask you to wear many hats. You will be thinking like an occupational therapist, an eye doctor, even a neuroscientist, as I introduce basic concepts of the muscular, visual and nervous systems. Understanding these concepts will help you know why these techniques and strategies work. (While my focus is primarily in the area of piano and keyboards, many of these techniques can be applied to general music education as well as other instruments.) Hopefully these recommendations will inspire you to develop unique programs for your own special-needs students.

According to the United States Census Bureau, there are 51.2 million people who have a disability, 11 percent of which are children—or approximately 4 million. The term "disability" refers to a disturbance in an individual's ability to function, which includes physical or sensory impairment, cognitive impairment or a mental disorder.

The National Association for Music Education (MENC) embodies approximately 130,000 members, who include music teachers, university faculty, researchers and college music students. This does not take into account the number of music educators not associated with MENC. With such a large number of educators, one would think that there should be enough teachers to accept those disabled individuals who want to learn music. However, whether it be due to lack of training, perception of a disabled person's capabilities or an understandable hesitancy to accept a student who will prove more challenging than most, there is a shortage of teachers who are willing to take on a special-needs individual as a student—especially in a private, one-to-one session. I have seen this great need personally over my years of teaching and have received many requests from parents across North America who want their disabled children to learn how to play the piano but cannot find a teacher equipped to accept such a student. Sadly, I often must turn these families down due to time constraints or geographic logistics. But even more disheartening is the fact that I am typically at a loss in giving these parents a recommendation of a like-minded music educator to contact.

Why is this the case? A fellow private music instructor, Anabela Rossi, believes that it may have something to do with our own desire to observe success in our students. "How do we, as teachers, define success?" she asks. "We want our students to learn, but many times we have preconceived notions about how to measure that learning. And to adjust that 'measurement' for every child would be an investment, but as with any investment we make in life, monetary or non-monetary, *our* motivation is the reward, which seems to be much simpler when you're talking about a disabled person."

For the individual with a disability, the success may be subtle, even inconsequential, by our standards. However, by the standards of our student with the disability and his family, this "subtle" success may be one of the single most important achievements of his life.

If this book does one thing, I want it to inspire you to teach just one person with special needs—and empower you with the knowledge and the confidence to take on this important and rewarding challenge. Go and find your own "Summer." Take it from me: It will change your life. For the better.

Chapter 1

The Occupation of the Musician: We Are What We Do

Like you, I am a musician. I started taking formal piano lessons at age 5 and continue taking lessons to this day. Education is a life-long process; there is always more to be learned. I am also an occupational therapist. The word "occupation" is an often-misunderstood word. For those unfamiliar with the term, realize that I do *not* find people jobs. (A client once said to me, "Honey, I'm 90 years old. I'm not looking for a job.") "Occupation" refers to anything that people do within the course of their day. For adults, this may include: making meals, taking care of children, working or participating in hobbies/sports. The "occupation" of children may include: eating meals, playing, going to school or participating in hobbies/sports. However, if an individual has a disability, it may affect any of these "occupation" areas.

An occupational therapist's role is to help such individuals develop or restore their ability to perform skills necessary for their "occupation." There are instances when it is not possible to develop or restore the ability 100 percent. In those cases, the occupational therapist figures out a way to help the person be as independent as possible, processes that may include the use of adaptive devices or techniques.

Occupational therapists have medical backgrounds. Typical courses include: gross anatomy, neuroscience, kinesiology and a variety of psychology classes. We work in many public and private sectors, such as hospitals, school systems, nursing homes and psychiatric settings. We also consult for companies that need to reintegrate a newly disabled individual into his previous work setting. Our patients are faced with a variety of challenges and conditions: stroke or hip replacement recovery, amputations, cerebral palsy, Down syndrome, muscular dystrophy, Alzheimers, etc.

Our many psychology classes give us insight into what it may feel like to have a disability and, in turn, how to work with such individuals. We learn to listen and identify what is important to the patient. Sometimes things that we perceive as unimportant may mean the world to them. We also learn not to underestimate the power of motivation. One of our primary philosophies as a profession is that motivation is what drives a person to function. We typically look for what interests the patient and have him work on that specific task. And in performing that task, the individual may be working on the therapist's goals, such as increasing muscle strength, improving coordination and problem-solving. Something a woman said to me while I was a teenager volunteering in a hospital's occupational therapy department still resonates: "I like coming to occupational therapy. Physical therapy is okay, too, but I just do things like leg and arm exercises. In occupational therapy, I do things that I enjoy doing and I don't realize that I'm helping to strengthen my body when I do them."

Thus, for our purposes, an "occupation" may include playing music, providing the motivation is there. A person born with a disability may want to learn music. Or perhaps a person might have played music prior to developing a condition (post-stroke, brain injury, hand injury, etc.) and still want to play. Either motivation will drive improvements. While some disabled people learn as any "typical" student would, others may require special adaptations to help them learn.

This brings me to *my* motivation to write this book: I understand music; I understand the concepts of occupational therapy. Why not combine the two? I do not consider my practices "music therapy" per se, because I did not go to school for that discipline—a highly important profession unto its own. What I do is teach music using the standard methods we all have learned, but employ my occupational therapy background to adapt these lessons for my special-needs students' individual levels of comprehension and physical capabilities.

And in the course of this book, you will learn how to do the same.

Chapter 2

We Are All Musical:
The Special Types of People You May Meet

When discussing people with disabilities, we must always remember that they are people first. On the first day of my first occupational therapy class, I was reprimanded for this very slight. I had asked a question regarding a "disabled person" and my teacher firmly said, "You meant to say, 'a person with a disability.'" So: Person first; disability second.

There are many types of disabilities—so numerous that I cannot cover all of them within the confines of one chapter. Therefore, I will discuss the most common conditions that you may encounter while teaching music to a student with special needs.

Down Syndrome

Down syndrome occurs when a person is born with three, rather than two, copies of chromosome 21. This is why Down syndrome is also called "Trisomy 21." Physical characteristics include:

➤ Low muscle tone
➤ Flat facial profile
➤ Upward slant to the eyes
➤ Hyper-flexibility
➤ Weakness throughout the body

Individuals with Down syndrome also typically have a certain degree of mental retardation, which may fall within the "mild" to "moderate" range. It is important to remember that individuals with Down syndrome, like other disabilities, are able to develop and learn; they simply do so at a later age than their peers without this disorder. The majority are able to learn to sit, walk, talk, play, use the toilet and do most other activities that non-disabled individuals perform. For example, a child without Down syndrome typically starts walking unassisted between 9 and 18 months; a Down syndrome child starts walking between 1 and 4 years. And a non-Down syndrome child starts dressing himself on average between 3 1/2 and 5 years versus the Down syndrome child, who will reach this milestone between 3 1/2 and 8 1/2 years.

Cerebral Palsy

Cerebral palsy is a chronic condition that affects the ability to move the body and coordinate muscles. Damage to one or more areas of the brain either during fetal development, around the time of birth or during infancy and early childhood may result in this condition. The damage alters the brain's ability to voluntarily control movement and posture: It does not mean that muscles and nerves are damaged. Cerebral palsy can occur in a variety of degrees, from mild to moderate to severe. Certain individuals may not be able to talk or move their bodies at all, while others may have a subtle variation in the way that they walk or may simply not be as coordinated as their peers. Depending upon the area of the brain damaged, the following characteristics may be exhibited:

➤ Muscle tightness
➤ Involuntary movement
➤ Abnormal sensation/perception
➤ Difficulty in the senses of sight, hearing or speech
➤ Learning disabilities
➤ Mental retardation

Autism

Autism is a neurological disorder that impacts the development of the brain, particularly in the areas of social interaction and communication. Individuals with this disorder typically have difficulties with verbal and non-verbal communication, social interactions and play/leisure activities. Autism falls within the category of "Pervasive Developmental Disorders" (PDD), which includes five neurological disorders that are considered to be "severe and pervasive impairments in several areas of development" (DSM IV). Other areas that are categorized along with autism include Asperger's Disorder, Rett's Disorder, childhood disintegrative disorder and PDD-Not Otherwise Specified (PDD-NOS). Autism presents itself differently in each person and, like other disorders, can vary in degrees of severity. Characteristics may include:

➤ Little or no eye contact
➤ Resistance to change
➤ Echolalia (repetition of words)

➤ Preference to play/work alone

➤ Difficulty expressing wants/needs

➤ Tantrums

➤ Hyper- or hypo-sensitivity to sound, touch, pain

➤ Uncoordinated movement

➤ Poor responsiveness to verbal communication. (If verbal communication does not develop, individuals may employ sign language or pictures to communicate.)

While autistic individuals will not "grow out" of this disorder, their symptoms may decrease as they develop and receive appropriate treatment. One notable example is Dr. Temple Grandin. In addition to holding a Ph.D. in Animal Science, she has written a book, which I highly recommend, that discusses her experiences with autism: *Thinking in Pictures: And Other Reports From My Life With Autism* (Doubleday, 1995).

Attention Deficit Disorder

Attention Deficit Disorder is a common diagnosis for children who display inattention, hyperactivity and/or impulsivity. All children are at times normally restless, impulsive and succumb to daydreaming. They are *children* after all, and it is in their nature to be this way. However, when these characteristics consistently impact on the child's performance in school, social relationships or behavior, this diagnosis should be considered. There are two types of Attention Deficit Disorder. One is the basic Attention Deficit Disorder (ADD) and the other has the hyperactivity component—Attention Deficit Hyperactivity Disorder (ADHD). The child with ADHD is more likely to be identified as having this condition than the child with ADD, which can be more subtle. ADHD has more outward signs, such as uncontrolled restlessness during table-top tasks and behavior problems. The child with ADD is the daydreamer who looks out the window or doodles during a lesson and does not complete his schoolwork. These children often are thought of as "unmotivated" rather than having an underlying problem.

Here are some of the terminology associated with ADD and/or ADHD:

➤ **Hyperactivity.** These children incessantly are "on the go" or constantly in motion. They exhibit characteristics like excessive touching, talking or playing with toys for a short period of time, only to move onto the next activity. These children will shift in their seats during dinner or at school, or will need to move around the room. They may kick their feet under their desks, tap their pencils or otherwise fidget with items.

➢ **Impulsivity.** These children may be labeled as "discipline problems" when in reality they are simply unable to stop and think before they act. They are quick to exhibit emotions, may blurt out answers and have difficulty waiting their turns during social situations, such as game-playing. Instead of talking to peers about their feelings during a conflict, these children might rather hit.

➢ **Inattention.** These children are perceived as unmotivated. They become easily confused and tend to be slow-movers. Often, teachers will have to tell these children to hurry along. It may appear that they are paying attention in school or even working, though in reality, they may not be paying full attention to the teacher. They get bored quickly and are easily distracted by sights and sounds. Schoolwork is challenging as they may forget to write down assignments or may leave materials at school. Their homework is typically filled with errors, careless mistakes and erasure marks. They also may give their parents a difficult time about completing homework.

Tourette's Syndrome

People with Tourette's Syndrome have a variety of tics or repetitive mannerisms that typically emerge during times of nervousness or stress. These mannerisms may include excessive eye blinking, grimacing, throat clearing, sniffing, shouting obscenities or barking words. Tourette's Syndrome is often associated with ADHD and its behaviors can be controlled with medication. It is important to note that these individuals cannot help these tics. With a Tourette's student, it is best for the teacher to ignore his tics and just proceed with the lesson.

Sensory Integrative Dysfunction

Sensory Integrative Dysfunction (SID) is a relatively new diagnosis used to describe a condition where there is a miscommunication between the brain and one or more sensory system. Dr. A. Jean Ayres was an occupational therapist who first researched this area and wrote the book *Sensory Integration and the Child* (Western Psychological Services, 1979). According to Dr. Ayres, sensory information is like "food for the brain similar to the food which nourishes our physical bodies. Difficulty processing and organizing sensory information causes dysfunction which can be compared to indigestion which occurs when the digestive tract malfunctions." Should this "indigestion" occur, particular parts of the brain will not receive the sensory information that they need to perform their functions.

Again, Sensory Integrative Dysfunction presents on a continuum from "mild" to "severe" and may be remediated with development and treatment. The following are symptoms that may be present:

➤ Distractibility
➤ Impulsivity
➤ Over- or under-sensitivity to touch, movement, sounds or sights
➤ Clumsiness/carelessness
➤ Emotional and/or social problems
➤ Decreased self-esteem
➤ Difficulty calming down
➤ Abnormally high or low level of activity
➤ Delay in speech, language, academic or motor skills

The Out of Sync Child (The Berkley Publishing Group, 1998) by Carol Stock Kranowitz, M.A., is a highly recommended and reader-friendly resource for any parent or educator working with a child suspected of having sensory integrative dysfunction. It discusses sensory integrative dysfunction as well as details strategies to help cope with this condition.

Learning Disability

"Learning disability" is an umbrella term that refers to a neurological disorder affecting the ability to understand or use spoken or written language. Dyslexia is an example of a learning disability. Learning disability is often referred to as a "hidden" disability since individuals with learning disabilities may not look different from individuals without it. They are often bright people; however, they are unable to show their understanding at an age-appropriate level. Oftentimes, these individuals may have a weakness in one area, such as reading and spelling, but may have a strength in math, art or science. Most people with learning disabilities have average or above-average intelligence, but will be challenged continually throughout their lives to adapt their learning processes. However, given the right amount of support and understanding, these people can become successful in school, work, relationships and their community.

Central Auditory Processing Disorder

Central Auditory Processing Disorder is an example of a learning disability. I want to discuss this one in particular because it is highly possible that you will encounter a student with this condition. This disorder causes difficulty with processing and remembering language-based tasks. (Music lessons are a perfect example of a language-based task.) Here are some symptoms that are related to this condition:

➢ May be able to interpret or recall non-verbal sounds, such as music

➢ Difficulty explaining thoughts and ideas

➢ Slow processing time (responds slower to questions, needs to think for a longer period of time before responding)

➢ Distracted by noise

➢ Difficulty paying attention

➢ Difficulty following verbal multi-step directions (i.e. "Place your left hand on the C chord and with your right hand, strum the second, fourth and fifth strings.")

➢ Will ask "What?" even when it appears the person has heard much of what was said

➢ Difficulty comprehending complex sentences or rapid rate of speech

This information should give you a snapshot of some disabilities you might encounter. If a special-needs student approaches you for lessons, you should research his condition more and spend some time with the parents/caregiver in order to fully understand the strengths and challenges of the individual.

Chapter 3

The Role of Vision: How the Eyes Hold the key

L et's become eye professionals for one moment. The eye works much like a camera. (Fig. 01.) Light enters through the outer, dome-like portion (the cornea) and continues through the pupil. The lens transmits and focuses images on the retina (like film in a camera). The macula "fine tunes" the images—much like a professional photographer does with a camera—allowing sharp, precise vision for tasks such as reading and driving. After the fine-tuning is complete, the retina sends the image through the optic nerve to the brain for visual processing to occur. Visual processing allows us to recognize and interpret information retrieved from our sense of vision.

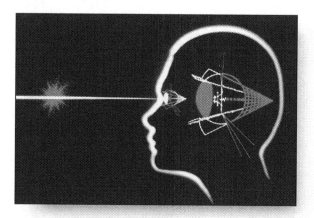

Fig.01

Oftentimes individuals diagnosed with learning disabilities will demonstrate difficulty in the area of visual processing, which places them at a disadvantage since so much of our daily information is presented visually. Therefore, there are two problems that may occur within the visual system:

1. Ability to see or see with clarity
2. Ability to process what is seen

The following are examples of visual dysfunctions:

Myopia (nearsightedness): inability to clearly see distant objects. According to "Healthy People 2010," a set of health objectives developed by Federal agencies, approximately 25 percent of the U.S. population has myopia. Myopic individuals have eyeballs with an elongated shape. The light that normally passes through the lens directly to the retina is instead focused in front of it, distorting vision.

Hyperopia (farsightedness): inability to clearly see objects close to the field of vision. These individuals must make an effort to focus on an object. Headaches, eye strain and fatigue when focusing on near objects are symptoms of this condition. Hyperopic individuals have eyeballs that are shorter in shape. Images are focused behind the retina, which causes them to appear blurry.

Astigmatism: a combination of myopia and hyperopia as a result of an irregularly shaped cornea or lens resulting in varying degrees of blurred vision at all distances. While some individuals may have astigmatism and not notice it, others may complain of eyestrain, headaches or blurred/distorted vision. (Fig. 02.)

Fig.02

Even when an eye is completely healthy, the visual system still can be compromised by dysfunction in visual processing. Following are two areas of visual processing ability that are commonly used in music and may be affected by dysfunction:

1. Spatial relation: The ability to perceive the position of objects in their environment or "space" to perceive objects in "space" in relation to other objects. (Fig. 03.)

Fig.03

Here are two mathematical examples of spatial relations:

➤ Understanding that "17" is "seventeen" and not "1" and "7".

➤ Understanding that the "+" and "=" signs in the equation "4+5=" are distinct from the numbers, but that there is a relationship between them and that relationship must be understood to write in the answer to the equation.

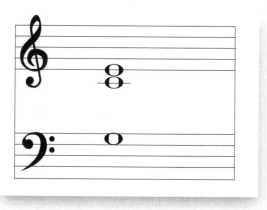

Fig.04

Here are two music examples of spatial relations:

➤ Understanding that the right hand plays Middle C and E at the same time that the left hand plays a G. (Fig. 04.)

➤ Understanding that a note placed on the second space of the treble clef is always an A.

2. Visual discrimination: Ability to differentiate objects based upon their distinct characteristics. This skill is necessary to identify common items and symbols. Identification may occur by using individual attributes, such as color, shape, size, texture, pattern or position. The ability to recognize an object within its environment is another example of a visual discrimination skill (think *Highlights* magazine). (Fig. 05.)

Fig.05

Here are two reading examples of visual discrimination:

➤ Ability to distinguish between the words "now" and "mow." "Now" has an "n" in the beginning, which has "one hump"; "mow" has an "m" in the beginning, which has "two humps."

➤ Ability to recognize letters written on a blackboard.

Here are two music examples of visual discrimination:

➤ Ability to interpret pre-reading music where numbers or letters are written within the note.

➤ Ability to recognize notes of different time values (i.e. quarter-note, half-note).

Individuals with the following medical conditions are at increased risk for vision problems:

➤ Developmental delay

➤ Premature birth

➤ Down syndrome

➤ Neurological conditions (i.e. post-stroke, cerebral palsy)

There are two types of eye doctors:

Ophthalmologist: a medical doctor who evaluates the health and integrity of the eye structure as well as performs corrective eye surgeries.

Optometrist: a doctor of optometry (not a medical doctor) who is able to diagnose vision problems and eye disease, prescribe eyeglasses/contact lenses and drugs to treat disorders of the eye. Optometrists often will evaluate the coordination of the eyes. They do not perform surgery.

It is possible for children to have serious vision problems without demonstrating any symptoms. Therefore, the American Academy of Pediatrics recommends that infants be screened during their checkups and that formal vision testing be performed annually for all children three years of age and older.

Now, let's return to being music educators. Many children start formal music lessons around the first grade. That is also the time when reading and writing are stressed more in school. Given these academic and extracurricular activities, children at this age are required to visually retrieve and process more information than they have up to this point. Symptoms of visual problems may become more apparent during this time. Therefore, it is important that teachers of all disciplines—music educators included—maintain a "watchful eye" on this issue and inform parents if a concern arises. Educators are often the first line of defense against vision problems. General symptoms of vision problems may include (but aren't limited to):

➤ Squints/closes one eye/rubs eyes

➤ Excessive blinking

➤ Fatigues quickly

➤ Complains of headaches, blurry vision

➤ Turns or tilts head in order to use one eye

➤ Favors one eye

➤ Exhibits postural problems, such as head-tilting or shoulder-hiking

➤ Bumps into objects, exhibits "clumsy" behavior

The symptoms that are specific to music education may include (but aren't limited to):

➤ Inability to see notes

➤ Inability to maintain visual attention to music (i.e. turning head away, easily distracted)

➤ Inability to visually follow notes horizontally or vertically
➤ Inability to resume place in music after looking down at instrument
➤ Uses finger to read music
➤ Frequently loses place in music or skips notes
➤ Positions head close to music

Frustration is also an important symptom to note. A student may exhibit behaviors, such as putting his head down on table, complaining that he hates music, crying or becoming non-responsive. Should this occur, it is important to talk to your student about his feelings. There is the possibility that he may not even recognize that his problem is due to visual difficulty. In that case, it is up to you to try some of the visual adaptations suggested in Chapter 7.

Jacyln's Story

One of my students, "Jacyln," who has cerebral palsy, began piano lessons at age seven because she wanted to learn music and needed to work on developing her hand/finger coordination. Though she began lessons as any typical student, eventually her interest significantly waned. She would put her head on the piano, bang the keys and even tell me that she "hates piano" and wanted to know "when lessons would be over—for good." I discussed the situation with Jacyln's mother, and we decided to continue and just keep encouraging her. She often refused to practice at home, which was part of the problem.

Everything changed, however, when I brought in enlarged sheet music for her lessons. Jacyln told me that the notes were much easier for her to read on these sheets, and as each lesson progressed, her negative behaviors decreased. Though lessons were still a challenge for her because of difficulty with coordination, she was better able to develop her coordination when she actually could see the notes in front of her. And then when she started playing music by Alicia Keys, one of her favorite musicians, her coordination improved even more. That is a result of a key component in my process—motivation.

Chapter 4

The Muscular System: The Power Behind the Desire

Now, let's take a crash course in gross anatomy and learn how our muscles work. This will enable us to understand why individuals with disabilities may have a difficult time physically coordinating their movements while playing music. We also will learn why it may be important to incorporate "warm-up" exercises or music adaptation to allow the greatest independence and ability for each student.

First and foremost, the student must have a desire to move: a desire to strum a chord on the guitar, bang a drum or play a descending arpeggio on the piano. Without motivation, muscles will not be called to action by the brain. Consider this: You come home after a long, hard day only to be greeted with a pile of dirty dishes looming in the sink. You just want to take your shoes off, lie on the couch and unwind; you have no desire to attend to the dishes. Therefore, you don't. So, while you have the physical ability to clean the dishes, you have no desire to complete this task.

The same is true when it comes to music. Certain people have that desire to learn and play music. Others do not, and that is fine as well. Many individuals with disabilities have the same desire to learn and play music as their able-bodied peers. This desire encourages them to work through their physical difficulties (i.e. incoordination) to achieve their goal.

Robert, a 14-year-old with Down syndrome, is a perfect example of an individual with the desire to learn music. Underlying lower-than-average muscle tone causes Robert to work harder than others to coordinate the movements of his hands and fingers. When he first learned how to play notes with different fingers, he often would depress two notes instead of the one that he was attempting to play. For example, when trying to play an F with his fourth finger, Robert would play an E as well. He is able to recognize when he makes this mistake and independently works on that section of his song until he only plays the F. His desire helps to build strength and coordination in his hand.

Now, let's discuss how our muscles work. There are three types of muscles: skeletal, smooth and cardiac.

For the purpose of this book, we will concentrate on skeletal muscles, which are those that we can see and feel. (Fig. 06.) When we exercise, we work on increasing skeletal muscle mass. Examples include biceps, triceps, quadriceps and abdominal muscles. These types of muscles attach to the skeleton and typically contract voluntarily. The primary action of these muscles is contraction. Muscles can do a short, single contraction (known as "twitch") or a long and sustained contraction (known as "tetanus"). A twitch may occur when playing a staccato note on the piano. Playing a G Major chord sustained for four beats is an example of tetanus contraction. (Fig. 07.)

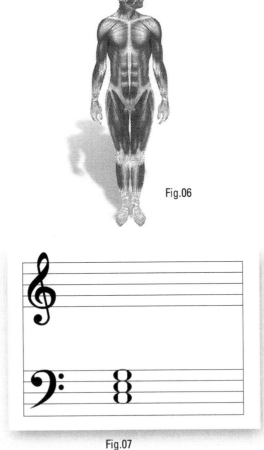

Fig.06

Fig.07

Let's say that you want to move your arm to pick up a glass of water, an effort that primarily involves your biceps muscle. Once you decide to pick up the glass, the brain transmits an electrical signal (action potential) down to a nerve cell, causing it to release a chemical message (neurotransmitter) into a small space (synapse) between the nerve cell and the muscle cell. When enough action potentials are present, the biceps muscle is instructed to contract.

These electrical signals (action potentials) and chemical messages (neurotransmitters) are integral players in the muscular system. There are three primary neurotransmitters: dopamine, norepinephrine and epinephrine. Dopamine is generally involved with motor planning and execution of movements as well as regulation of high-level sensory and motor processing (which will be discussed in Chapter 5). Should there be an impairment in the dopamine circuitry, a movement disorder may occur. Examples include Tourette's Syndrome and Parkinson's Syndrome. Norepinephrine and epinephrine (more commonly known as adrenaline) are important to assume and maintain arousal and attention. Impairment in the norepinephrine/epinephrine circuitry may lead to sleep and/or psychiatric disorders. It is impossible to learn about the role of the neurotransmitters without also learning about the role of the nervous systems, which will be discussed in Chapter 5.

But first, let's discuss the issue of muscle tone. Muscle tone is the state of activity or tension of a muscle or its active resistance to stretch. Everyone is born with a certain amount of muscle tone. There are individuals with high muscle tone and those with low muscle tone. Individuals with high muscle tone tend to have tighter bodies, which are harder to stretch. Individuals with low muscle tone tend to have looser bodies, which respond easily to stretch. The remainders fall within the average range, which includes high-average muscle tone or low-average muscle tone. It is important to note that the amount of muscle tone you are born with is the amount of muscle tone you have for life. You cannot increase or decrease it regardless of how much exercise you do. This is different from muscle strength, which you can watch develop as you do push-ups, swim or lift weights.

The person with high muscle tone has too many fibers activating muscles at the same time and therefore may not be able to control his movements. Individuals with severe cases of cerebral palsy are an extreme example. Stretching, often called "range of motion," of the body is often done by therapists; however, after a short duration, muscles in individuals with this severe condition will tighten up again and not allow functional movements.

Individuals with high muscle tone may exhibit the following:

➢ Difficulty moving arms/hands/fingers

➢ Tightness (fingers may be curved somewhat at the end)

➢ Difficulty playing with dynamics—inability to control the amount of pressure placed on instrument

The person with low muscle tone has too few fibers activating muscles, and therefore a great amount of energy is required to move the body. Individuals with Down syndrome are an example. Consider lifting a glass of water. Those with average muscle tone have no difficultly bringing it to their mouths to drink. Those with low muscle tone, however, have to recruit more muscle fibers to lift the glass; therefore it may feel like a workout after a few "repetitions" of raising the glass to their mouth.

Individuals with low muscle tone may exhibit the following:

➢ Soft/doughy muscles

➢ Rounded back posture while sitting in chair

➢ Difficulty keeping head in upright position

➢ Open mouth posture/drooling

If muscle tone cannot be increased or decreased, then what can be done to help these people develop the skill to play music? It's easier than you might think: People with high-average muscle tone need to relax their muscles, and people with low-average muscle tone need to "wake up" their muscles. Think about your routine before you start playing Chopin's "Etude," rock climb or any other activity involving a great deal of muscular strength, coordination and endurance. You may roll your neck, stretch out your legs, arms and hands, jump up and down a few times or eat an energy bar. These are your warm-ups. People with differences in muscle tone especially require similar warm-ups in order to perform at their optimal capacity.

There are times when the individual plays music seemingly to his fullest capacity and is not satisfied or making progress. There also are times when the individual physically cannot perform certain movements. Those are the situations where you will need to be creative and adapt the music to the ability of the person. For example, a student with one arm would not be expected to play standard two-handed piano music. Rather, he would use one-handed piano music. The same is true for individuals with muscular difficulties. Ways to adapt music for these special students and warm-ups that they can perform will be discussed in Chapter 7.

Chapter 5

The Nervous System: A Not-So-Simple Game of "Telephone"

There is much communication going on within our nervous systems. And just like in the children's game "Telephone," the more messengers you have involved, the greater the chance of something getting lost in the translation. Conditions such as autism, attention deficit/attention deficit hyperactivity disorders, Sensory Integrative Dysfunction and learning disabilities may be a result of miscommunication within the nervous system.

When designing a music program for special-needs individuals, it's important to be aware of the nervous systems as they relate to these students. We have two nervous systems, both of which work together: the central nervous system and the peripheral nervous system. The central nervous system consists of the brain and the spinal cord, and it plays a fundamental role in the control of behavior. The peripheral nervous system consists of sensory neurons and motor neurons. Sensory neurons receive information from a stimulus and inform the central nervous system (brain and spinal cord) of this stimuli. Motor neurons receive the information from the brain and/or spinal cord and bring it to the muscles and glands so that action can occur. Here is an everyday example of this process in action: You are walking barefoot on the beach and all of the sudden you feel a sharp piece of glass under your foot (stimulus). Sensory neurons send the pain information to your brain and/or spinal cord. The motor neurons are sent down to the muscles of your leg and foot, which cause you to pick your foot off of the glass and shout "ouch!" Or when you touch a hot tea kettle, you yank your hand away (Fig. 08).

For the purpose of this section, we will concentrate on the peripheral nervous system, which is divided into two categories: the autonomic nervous system and the sensory-somatic nervous system. The autonomic nervous system helps individuals adapt to changes within their environment. It has the ability to adjust or modify the body in response to stress. Specifically, it helps to control blood pressure, electrical activity of the heart, air flow in the lungs and movement/action of the stomach. Following is an example of a typical autonomic nervous system at

Fig.08

work: You are in the middle of a business presentation, but your thoughts suddenly drift to your child who is home sick, the bills that are due and the groceries you need to pick up before you go home today. A colleague asks you a question and you realize that you have lost focus. Your heart races and your hands become sweaty. Because you have a typical autonomic nervous system, you are able to quickly regain composure and confidently answer your colleague's question. Conversely, an individual with an atypical autonomic nervous system would not be able to recover from such a situation. It would be extremely difficult for such an individual to even stand up in front of other people and speak.

The autonomic nervous system is divided into the sympathetic and parasympathetic nervous systems. The sympathetic nervous system accelerates heart rate, raises blood pressure and tightens muscles. The parasympathetic nervous system does the opposite: It slows heart rate, lowers blood pressure and relaxes muscles.

Let's correlate the autonomic nervous system to the example of a musical performance. You are on stage performing Moussorgsky's "Pictures at an Exhibition" from memory in front of a hall of approximately 100 people—and you play an obvious wrong note, a true lemon. It happens so quickly—your heart starts to race and you sense tension in the back of your neck as you try your best to recover (sympathetic nervous system). Then, you recall from your musical training a simple concept, one especially applicable to performance: "Don't forget to breathe." As you take in some deep, cleansing breaths, you find yourself back on track with your piece.

You also sense that your heart rate is slowing down and the tension in your neck seems to be resolving (parasympathetic nervous system).

The sensory-somatic nervous system is comprised of 12 pairs of cranial nerves and 31 pairs of spinal nerves, which may be sensory or motor in function or mixed.

Examples of cranial nerves are:

➤ **Ocularmotor nerve:** controls movement of the eyelid and eyeball muscles

➤ **Olfactory:** the sense of smell

➤ **Auditory:** the senses of hearing and balance

➤ **Optic:** the sense of vision

Examples of spinal nerves are:

➤ **Cervical spinal nerves:** signals sent to/from the neck, back of the head, shoulders, arms/hands, diaphragm

➤ **Thoracic spinal nerves:** signals sent to/from the chest, some muscles in the back and abdomen

An individual with an impairment of the sensory-somatic nervous system can have manifestations in a variety of different ways dependent upon which nerve is affected. For example, damage to the ocular-motor nerve may cause pain and/or loss of vision. Damage to the olfactory nerve may cause a loss or distortion of the smell sensation, which can impair the ability to detect environmental hazards (i.e. natural gas, smoke, spoiled food). Spinal nerve damage may cause pain and/or loss of movement of the muscles, which the nerves stimulate.

When teaching a music lesson, we assume that our student is looking, listening and feeling what we are trying to impart. This would be true for the student with a typical nervous system; however, we must first consider these basic needs are met for the student with atypical nervous systems. The following are a few considerations that you should take into account prior to educating this type of student or if you have a student you believe it having difficulty learning in general:

1. Eye contact: Learning is best done when eye contact is first established.

2. Proper seating: Learning is best done when the student is comfortable.

3. Rate of speech: Learning is best done when the student can clearly understand what the teacher is saying.

4. Limit outside distractions: Close the door, move to a room with less noise filtering inside.

Once these factors are considered and addressed, the student's nervous system should be prepared to learn. Next we must consider what to do when the nervous system we are dealing with in the lesson is not capable of allowing the individual to learn in the most effective manner. Perhaps we have to tap into more than one sensory system. This is known as the multisensory approach to learning.

Chapter 6

Coming to Our Senses:
The "Multisensory Learner" in All of Us

I was once asked to observe a colleague's piano lesson with a child who had special needs. During this observation, the piano teacher told me that her student was labeled by the parent as a "multisensory learner." My initial reaction was: Who is *not* a multisensory learner?

Considering the way I learned in school, I would also fall into this category—as would many of you. In my case, I have a tendency to get tired quickly when I read, especially when I'm reading dry textbooks. To compensate for this problem, I not only read the information but I also take written notes, make flashcards and record comments into a dictation machine so I can listen to them while driving. While dictating, however, I do not speak in monotone; rather, my voice is enthusiastic.

Thus, following are the various systems I personally use while studying:
➤ Visual system: reading notes
➤ Visual system, auditory system: reading notes aloud
➤ Visual system, auditory system (if answers are verbalized): flashcards
➤ Visual system, proprioceptive system (see page 28): writing notes
➤ Auditory system: listening to notes in car

Here is some background about each sense. Individuals with difficulties in any of these sensory areas are often referred to as having "sensorimotor" problems:
➤ Auditory sensation refers to the ability to hear.
➤ Visual sensation refers to the ability to see.
➤ Gustatory sensation refers to the sensation that results when the taste buds in the mouth and throat receive information about the taste of something placed in the mouth.
➤ Tactile sensation refers to the sensation produced by pressure receptors in the skin in response to touch.
➤ Vestibular sensation refers to the sensation in response to movement.
➤ Olfactory sensation refers to the sensation that results when olfactory receptors within the nose are stimulated by chemicals in the air. (Basically, the ability to smell.)

➤ Proprioception (or kinesthetic) sensation refers to the ability to sense the position, location and movement of the body and its parts. Proprioception is an integral component in the ability to learn, repeat and become comfortable with movements throughout life. Should this sensation be impaired, an individual would still be able to control muscular movement; however, he would have to use the sense of sight to understand where his limbs were or what they were doing.

Since proprioception is one of the less-obvious sensations, let's examine it a bit further. Say that you are teaching a beginner piano student who has an impaired proprioceptive sense due to a mild stroke suffered one year prior. This student is able to play Middle C easily; however, because he has difficulty with proprioception, he must constantly look down at the finger to determine what it is doing. Touch receptors and proprioceptive receptors are highly dependent upon one another. If there is an impairment in the sense of touch, the ability to sense the position of the limb is compromised. Similarly, if there is an impairment in the ability to sense the position of the limb, there is a decrease in the ability to interpret touch.

Here is an exercise to help you understand proprioception. Put two pairs of gloves on each hand. (Go ahead and actually do this because you will learn best by doing.) Next, take out any piece of music and play your instrument. How well do you do? What is your coordination like? Are you looking at your hands more often than usual? How well do you feel the instrument with your fingers? Are you getting frustrated? By doing this exercise you will never forget what an individual with impairment of the proprioceptive system deals with during music lessons.

What are our senses telling us?

Though an individual's senses may be functional on a basic level, there still may be sensorimotor problems. Think about what happens when you touch a hot tea kettle. First, you feel it (tactile sensation) and then you yank your hand away. Simple, right? Not quite. There is a very important component that occurs before you even yank your hand away. Your brain processes the information that you receive as you touch the kettle and decides subconsciously, or even reflexively, that you need to immediately remove your hand before it gets burned. If there is an impairment in processing this sensory information, there is the chance that you may leave your hand on the kettle, resulting in serious injury.

"Sensory processing" refers to the process by which the brain registers, organizes and interprets information from any of our sensory systems. Poor sensory processing can occur within any of the sensory systems: visual, olfactory, gustatory, tactile, proprioceptive/kinesthetic, vestibular or auditory. These individuals either under-react (hypo-respond) or over-react (hyper-respond) to stimuli, which affects their ability to pay attention, learn and perform.

An individual who demonstrates difficulty processing everyday sensory information is often referred to as having sensory processing disorder (SPD). This is a complex brain disorder that may lead to other problems, such as incoordination and behavioral issues. We all have a certain arousal state that fluctuates throughout the day from low to high levels of arousal. Here are some common examples:

High-Arousal State (hyper-responsiveness):
➤ Waking up at 7 a.m. when you are supposed to be checking in for an international flight by 7:15 a.m.
➤ Driving in icy conditions when you do not have all-wheel drive
➤ Hearing a bump in the night when you are alone in the house
➤ Getting ready to perform a solo recital at Carnegie Hall

Low-Arousal State (hypo-responsiveness):
➤ Lying on the beach under the warm sun
➤ Collapsing in bed after a long day
➤ Taking a warm bath
➤ Listening to a three-hour lecture on an uninteresting topic

From our personal experiences, we know that it is difficult to function when we are at a high-arousal state (hyper-responsive) or low-arousal state (hypo-responsive). Because we have normally functioning sensory and nervous systems, we are able to adjust our bodies to the "just right state" in order to function.

Now, let's take one example from each category to discuss how we typically adjust our bodies when we are at a high- or low-arousal state.

➤ Getting ready to perform a solo recital at Carnegie Hall. Obviously you feel like a giant ball of tension. It is difficult to focus on anything besides the fact that in three minutes you will be playing in front of a sold-out crowd. You are in a high-arousal state, and in order for you to play your best, you must get to the "just-right state." You close your eyes, put your head down and let your arms drop loosely to your sides. Then, you take a deep breath in and let it out. You repeat this breathing exercise several times. By the time you are introduced, you have brought your arousal state down and are able to walk onto the stage completely focused and ready to perform.

➤ Listening to a three-hour school lecture on the best way to control lint in the home. Unless you have sincere interest in lint, this would be torture. However, you must stay awake as your overall grade is based upon information contained within this lecture. You make it through by: doodling, taking notes, eating chewy, sugary foods, cracking your knuckles, taking occasional breaks to go to the bathroom or walk. Before you know it, the lecture is over and you feel confident that you absorbed enough information to pass the test.

Following are some symptoms of hyper-responsiveness in an individual:
➤ Responds to being touched with aggression or withdrawal
➤ Fears movement and heights or exhibits sickness resulting from exposure to movement or heights
➤ Exhibits caution or reluctance in taking on risks or trying new things
➤ Feels uncomfortable in loud or busy environments (i.e. malls, the circus)
➤ Is a picky eater and/or overly sensitive to food smells

The following are examples of symptoms of hypo-responsiveness in an individual:
➤ Hyperactivity (as this individual seeks more sensation)
➤ Unawareness of touch or pain (it may look like this individual is exhibiting aggressive behavior because he may touch others too hard)
➤ Involvement in unsafe activities, such as climbing too high
➤ Enjoying sounds that are excessively loud or making loud mouth sounds

As you can appreciate from your experience playing your instrument with two pairs of gloves, individuals with Sensory Integrative Dysfunction can easily become stressed, frustrated and oftentimes will develop negative attitudes toward school, extracurricular activities and, of course, music lessons. Rather than being a positive experience, learning is viewed as a constant struggle with little reward. Teachers and family members, not recognizing this struggle, might suggest that the individual is "not working up to his potential" or is "lazy" or "difficult" when in actuality, this may be the individual's maximum potential. It may be difficult for such a person to keep up with peers physically, socially and academically, which could lead to teasing and ultimately to low self-esteem. These individuals may suffer from conditions such as anxiety, depression or other behavioral problems. People who are unaware of this less-obvious handicap may even blame the parents for their children's "bad behavior."

This brings us to the title of this chapter: "The Multisensory Learner in All of Us." We all learn differently. Some learn best by listening to recorded lectures while taking a power walk, others by making flashcards, still others by color-coded notes. Consider the way that you learned your "ABCs." Chances are that you did not learn the sequence by just repeating it verbally. You probably learned the "ABC" song. Perhaps your teacher even made up a dance for the class to do while singing the song. If so, your teacher was addressing the "multisensory" learning needs of your classroom. Singing helped the auditory and visual learners, while the dance helped the proprioceptive/kinesthetic learners as well as the visual learners.

The best way to learn is to engage as many senses as possible. This concept is often overlooked during music lessons. The standard music lesson is a half-hour to one hour of sitting (or standing) with the instrument, listening to the teacher and reading/performing music. Then the student goes home to sit/stand with the instrument and practice. Of course, there are exceptions, but most people cannot devote 100 percent of their attention during a half-hour or one-hour music lesson. This is especially so in the case of individuals with disabilities.

Following are indicators that you have lost the attention of your student and need to do something to get it back:

➤ Decreased eye contact
➤ Talking about another topic
➤ Fidgeting
➤ Glazed look
➤ Student responding before you complete your directions
➤ Crying

We all ask our students, "Do you understand?" However, you should not always take "yes" for an answer. Instead, have the student show or tell you what they know. Here are some ideas to maintain your student's interest:

➤ Role play: "O.K., now you pretend that you are the teacher and I am the student. Can you tell me what an eighth note looks like and how I count it?"

➤ Use theory books. These provide an opportunity for teachers to actually see what the student understands.

➤ Clap out a rhythm.

➤ Write concepts within music, such as writing in counts under/over notes, circling all the eighth notes, writing flats/sharps in front of designated notes.

If you try these techniques and the student is unable to show or tell you what they know, chances are that they do not understand the concept. You then have a choice of either verbally explaining the concept again or taking "Plan M: The Multisensory Approach."

Chapter 7

Plan M:
The Multisensory Approach

Now that you have the theoretical background, let's work on the practical application. On the following pages, I will list a musical concept and then give practical multisensory strategies that you can use to help your student learn. I derived these strategies from occupational therapy concepts, from observing other professionals and from my own experiences. (While many of these concepts are related specifically to piano instruction, most can be incorporated when teaching other instruments.) Later in the chapter, I will discuss the concepts of warm-ups and the use of fidgets.

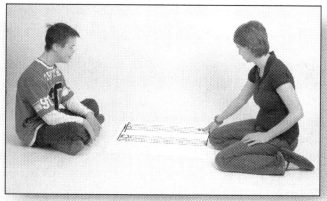

Fig.09

The suggestions that follow will inspire you to devise your own methods. And sometimes, your students will come up with their own ways of learning. Make sure you listen to what they say—you may learn something as well.

Reading Notes
Learning to read notes traditionally may not be the most enjoyable aspect of music education. Similar to learning multiplication tables, it

comes down to strict memorization of note names or intervals. Following are a few methods that make learning to read notes fun:

➤ *Color-By-Note* series (Books 1 and 2), by Sharon Kaplan (Alfred Publishing)

➤ *Color-By-Interval* series, by Sharon Kaplan (Alfred Publishing)

➤ *Dot-to-Dot Note Speller*, by Lisa Bastien (Neil A. Kjos Music Company)

➤ *Theory for Young Musicians, Notespeller* by Carla Ulbrich (Alfred Publishing).

➤ "Toss-a-Note" game: Draw a grand staff on a large piece of cardboard and take turns with your student tossing a chip onto the board. Wherever the chip lands, you must read the note (Fig. 09).

➤ "P-I-A-N-O": This game is based upon "B-I-N-G-O." Draw a game board consisting of five rows and five columns. (You can add more rows and columns as desired and call it "K-E-Y-B-O-A-R-D" or use the child's name.) Then, draw notes in each of the boxes. You can tailor the game to the specific student by drawing in target notes. (For example, if the student is having a difficult time reading Middle D, then you should draw a few Middle D's in the game board.) Cut out square "chips" with corresponding notes on them to place on the board (Fig. 10). Student and teacher then take turns picking up a "chip" and if they are able to read the note, they place it on their game board. For advanced "P-I-A-N-O" players: If someone reads a note wrong, the other player can "steal" the note by stating that it is incorrect and providing the correct letter name. Teachers, you can try to "trick" your students by naming the letter incorrectly. Students love to "steal" the letters from their teacher—but they have to say the letter correctly first!

➤ Note "Fortune-Teller": Make a "fortune-teller" out of paper (Fig. 11) and draw a note on a staff for each section. Have the student select the section by naming the note. On the innermost part of the fortune-teller, write a fortune. The student will have to read two notes in order to receive his "fortune."

Learning Notes on the Keyboard

➤ Velcro keyboard: Draw a keyboard; it can be two or more octaves (depending upon the size of the paper you choose) or can isolate a specific position, such as Middle C or Bass C. Then, on a separate piece of paper, write the corresponding letters. Laminate both and cut out the letters. Place sticky-back Velcro on the keyboard and the felt end on the back of each of the letters. Have your student stick the letters on top of the keys (Fig 12). You can try to "trick" the student by placing the letters on top of the wrong keys and see if he can play "teacher" and correct you.

Fig.10

Fig.11

➤ Star Wars: This song is a great way to learn where C is on the keyboard. A very simple adaptation (Faber) places two hands in Middle C position with the left hand occasionally crossing over the right to play a Treble C. The left hand can pretend to be a rocket ship blasting off to C! Sometimes the student can even travel farther into the "universe" by playing the next-highest C. Creative students can experiment with what it

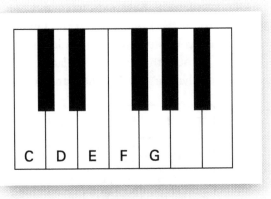

Fig.12

would sound like if the "rocket ship" left hand would play a Low C. As soon as the student understands the location of the C and that it can be found throughout the keyboard, it becomes easier to teach other notes.

➤ Place number or letter stickers on keys: I use this only as a last resort, especially when I'm dealing with a student with behavioral problems or one who has a tendency to become easily frustrated. When dealing with this circumstance, the goal is to have the student be successful and want to come back to the next lesson. As appropriate, start removing letters from the keyboard. Make it a big deal, something very exciting for the student. That way, there is a better chance that the student will remember the occasion and, hopefully, the note on the keyboard.

Note Values

➤ Rhythm "Fortune-Teller": This is similar as the note fortune-teller, only with the rhythm fortune-teller, you'd write notes of different values on the inside and have the student choose each by stating the type of note as well as the value (i.e. quarter note = one beat).

➤ Simon Says: The teacher claps a rhythm and the student claps it back. The teacher can make it more complex by adding in a snap or a tap on the head along with the clapping rhythm.

➤ Tap/Clap/Snap: I highly recommend learning rhythms away from the piano, especially if they are difficult. That may involve tapping the fingers on top of the piano or clapping the rhythm. It is fun to choose a certain activity to perform with each note value (Fig. 13, Fig. 14). For example, all quarter notes must be tapped on top of the piano. Half notes are snapped for their full value (one snap for one half note). Whole notes require the student to put his hands on his head and keep them there for the full value. Have the student choose what to do with each note value. Start out slow and then progress up to the correct beat.

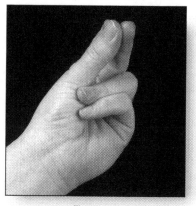

Fig.13

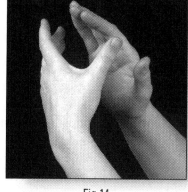

Fig.14

Left Vs. Right Hand

➢ L.H. and R.H.: In beginner piano books, these abbreviations often are used to signify left hand versus right hand while reading music. The student may not readily understand what they mean. Teach them. When introducing a new piece, point to the "L.H." or "R.H." and ask the student which hand plays.

➢ Stickers: Place a sticker with the letter L on the left hand and R on the right hand.

➢ Highlighter: Often, a visual reminder will help the student remember what hand should be playing. I typically trace the right-hand part with a pink highlighter and the left-hand part with a blue highlighter. This trains the student's eyes to play the right hand when looking at the top of the grand staff and to play the left when looking at the bottom of the grand staff. By the time he gets to music that may involve playing the right hand in the bass clef and left hand in the treble, the student should have no difficulty with this basic concept.

➢ Zoom: Enlarge music on photocopier so it is easier to read.

➤ Louds, softs and in-betweens all around us: Teach concepts by assimilating them to animals or environmental sounds. A soft, low sound may be a bear walking slowly through the forest. A loud, low sound may be a T-Rex stomping in the forest. A soft, high sound may be a bird. A soft, high sound with a quick staccato may be a butterfly. A train coming toward or away from us can be simulated by doing a sequence of crescendo followed by a diminuendo. Then ask the student to make a sound on the instrument and you guess what it may be.

Making Music Musical

➤ The ice-cream cone (Fig. 15): It is great when a music teacher tells a student that he knows the piece and can move on to learn another one. It is even better when the student is able to tell the teacher that he really knows how to play the piece and enjoys doing it or can independently talk about what needs to be improved. Oftentimes, music teachers move quickly through pieces before they become musical. Though it may be technically correct, it may not be played with emotion. I learned a great learning tool from music educator Patricia Thel at Westminster Choir College in Princeton, New Jersey, that involves the concept of an ice-cream cone: Make a large ice-cream cone out of construction paper and elaborate it according to the student's performance, using: a

Fig. 15

cone, three scoops of ice cream, hot fudge sauce, whipped cream, sprinkles and, of course, the cherry on top. Each "layer" signifies the way that the piece was played. The cone and one scoop of ice cream means that the piece is O.K., but requires many more "toppings." Three scoops mean it is really good, but there are some things still missing. Hot fudge and whipped cream make it amazing. Sprinkles mean the student played it like none other you have ever heard play it. The student who receives the "cherry on the top" has significantly changed the life of the teacher forever by playing that one piece. Of course, you can alter the meanings of each "topping." Have the student discuss what he or she feels should make up the ice-cream cone based upon the performance and ask the student put together the ice-cream cone based upon this discussion. It is a great way to actually "see" and measure progress.

Warm-Ups

Warm-ups are important for all of us. We do it before we rock climb, swim, take a long hike. Why not warm-up before we play music? Musicians use their muscles often with great intensity and speed. Concentration is more on fine motor skills, such as playing a trill on the piano, a pizzicato on the violin or holding a mallet to strike the marimba in a specified pattern.

Warm-ups are important for individuals with physical disabilities, such as Down syndrome or cerebral palsy. It is an opportunity to stretch out and strengthen the muscles, as well as to "wake them up" to get them ready to play.

It is also important to get our minds warmed up to play. Think about how you feel after you exercise: Your mind is clear, you have answers to problems or questions that were plaguing you throughout the day and you are more focused. You also feel energized. That is the result of endorphins in your body. These endorphins will be one of your greatest assets as you sit down to practice.

An individual with a condition such as attention deficit, Sensory Integrative Dysfunction or autism will need this "kick" to get his endorphins going in order to focus during the lesson. One to two minutes of these warm-ups at the start of the lesson will get his body ready. It is important to notice when the student may be showing signs of decreased focus during the lesson. That may signal that it is time to do another one to two minutes of these warm-ups to keep him going for the rest of the lesson.

It is important to discuss these warm-up activities with the parents and explain the reasons why you do them. Most individuals should be able to participate in exercises; however, there are conditions, such as Brittle Bone Disease or those involving contractures of arms, hands or fingers, for which these warm-ups may be contraindicated. If the student is receiving occupational or physical therapy, you can contact the therapist for approval of particular warm-ups.

Following are some suggestions for warm-up activities. It is generally best to start out with large muscles (shoulder/arm) and then work down to smaller muscles (wrists/hands/fingers).

➢ Arm rolls: forward and backward
➢ Head/neck rolls (Fig. 16, Fig. 17)

Fig.16

Fig.17

Fig.18

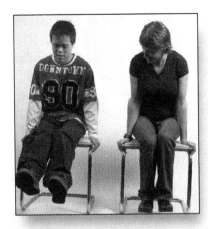

Fig.19

Fig.20

Fig.21

Fig.22

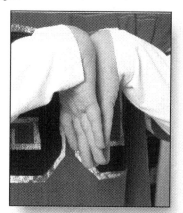

Fig.23

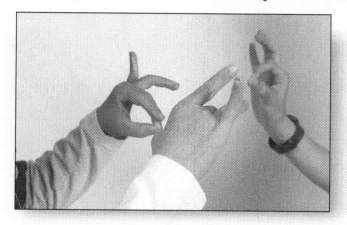

Fig.24

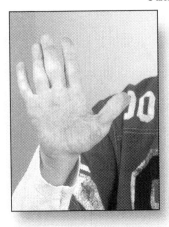

Fig.25

Fig.26

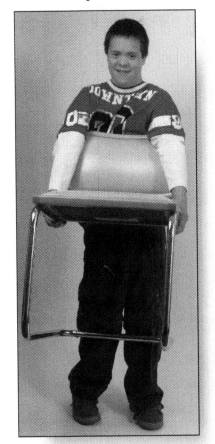

Fig.27

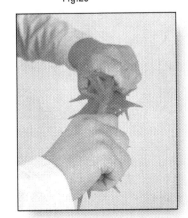

Fig.28

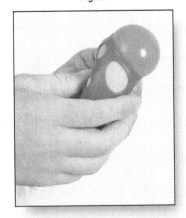

Fig.29

➢ Shoulder shrugs: Tense up the body for five seconds, then release (Fig. 18)

➢ Chair push-ups (Fig. 19)

➢ Wall push-ups (Fig. 20)

➢ Shadowing: Student places his hands on yours; tell him to push into your hands while you move your hands around (Fig. 21)

➢ Push two hands into each other, palms together (Fig. 22)

➢ Push two hands into each other, back sides together (Fig. 23)

➢ Wrist rolls: forward and backward

➢ Finger pushes: Take turns pushing each finger into the thumb of that hand-pointer finger and thumb, middle finger and thumb, ring finger and thumb, pinky and thumb (Fig. 24)

➢ Finger spread: Spread fingers wide, hold for five seconds, then release (Fig. 25)

➢ Open/close hands: Squeeze hands hard into a fist, hold for five seconds, then extend them as much as possible (Fig. 26)

➢ Heavy work: carry a chair, a few books, push bench in/out (Fig. 27)

Fidgets: What they are and how can they be used

A fidget is a word to describe an item we can use to keep our hands and fingers busy while we are concentrating. You probably are unaware that you use fidgets every day. Here are some common examples:

➢ Snapping the cap of a pen

➢ Doodling

➢ Playing with keys in a pocket

➢ Picking at fingers

➢ Tapping fingers on a desk

➢ Taking apart a paper clip

➢ Snapping a rubber band

Think about when you do these kinds of fidgets—during lectures, conversing, waiting in line—and you'll notice they are times when you may be bored or you have to sustain your attention. Individuals with disabilities need these fidgets as well; however, oftentimes they are unable to locate their own fidget or may do so by doing more disruptive things, such as squirming or kicking their feet under their chairs. Or you may feel that you are losing their attention when you attempt to teach them a concept.

In that case, the solution is the fidget box. Be creative when compiling your fidget box. Put in squeezy stress balls, rubber band balls, coiled key chains, bendable figures and a few linked paper clips. A trip to the dollar store will produce a treasure-trove of goodies for your fidget box. *Pocket Full of Therapy* is a wonderful therapy supply catalog that sells a variety of unusual squeeze balls as well as a full fidget kit. Allow the student to select one fidget to use during the lesson when it is time to listen (Fig. 28, Fig. 29). Put the fidget down when it is his turn to play. Then return it to the box for the next week.

Chapter 8

The Role of the Family: How to Help Your Budding Musician Succeed

When I was a child practicing the piano, my grandmother, "Bam," would set the timer for 30 minutes and sit in the living room with me. She did not sit in the room to make sure that I abided by the timer that clocked my daily session. Instead, she sat and *listened*. She honestly enjoyed listening to me play "Crunchy Flakes" and "Which Witch is Which." This attention made my time at the piano very special and in a lot of ways this memory continues to encourage me to play to this day.

In these days of parents working late, quick dinners and activity/homework overload, there may not be a lot of time to practice music. The most unfortunate thing is that with limited amount of time also comes a limited amount of opportunities for families to sit and listen to their young musicians play.

I tell all of my students, even those with special needs, that they must make a commitment to practice every day—especially the day of the lesson, while the information is fresh in their memories. This routine ensures that the lesson will stick for the rest of the week. To help establish a routine, the student should set a consistent time each day specifically for music practice. If there happens to be a limited amount of time to practice on a certain day, the child should play for at least 10 minutes to get his fingers moving and to keep his mind musically active.

The student with special needs will require more assistance when practicing. For this reason, I encourage weekly contact with the family regarding what was learned in the lesson. For example, in some circumstances, I will invite parents to remain in the room for a lesson so that they can see how I teach the material. In essence, I am teaching them the lesson along with the student. The parents then can go home and reinforce the way that I taught the material. However, there are times when it may be unnecessary—or even detrimental—to have parents at the lesson. In these cases, I will stop the lesson five minutes early and discuss the material with the parents. Another strategy is to have my students give their parents "concerts" at the end of the lesson. That may involve my playing a duet with the student or having the student play solo. The students find this motivating, plus it is a good way to encourage them to work hard during the lesson. A final option is to audiotape the lesson. This allows the parents to learn the terminology I use and understand the way that I present the material so that they can do the same during the week. Since students often are motivated by listening to themselves play, I sometimes will play the recording during the lesson. Many students get so excited that they will listen to the tape on the ride home.

And that leads me to concerts. I highly recommend organizing concerts. Your students will work harder and learn their music better when they know that a concert is upcoming. A very important component of music lessons is learning how to perform in front of an audience, and concerts are an excellent way for students to learn how to cope with anxiety, build social skills (bowing, smiling) and increase self-esteem. Children with special needs have a greater propensity than other children to have low self-esteem. They may realize on some level that they are different than other people or may wonder why their bodies do not work as well as others. Therefore self-esteem is an essential area to address.

Playing concerts in front of accepting/familiar entities is a good place to start. Beginner piano students can play in front of their families, their pets or their stuffed friends. For more outgoing or composed students, try scheduling concerts at senior citizen complexes or nursing homes. The staffs are usually very welcoming to anyone who offers to entertain their residents.

And, yes, concerts *can* be performed by people with special needs. All of my students with special needs have participated in concerts, and some are now at the point where they exhibit no nervousness; some even act like hams. Families of individuals with special needs are especially proud when their children are able to entertain others. It is another way of mainstreaming people with special needs into the community. I also have found that such community involvement increases the empathy of "typically developing" music students when they watch and listen to these students play.

So my goal for this chapter can be summed up in one word: LISTEN. Encourage parents to listen to their children play. Make it a special time for the family. It is a good chance to slow down, relax and enjoy life. Consider that a special lesson from my Bam.

Chapter 9

Mission Possible:
Biographies of Special Musicians

Throughout the years I have taught many amazing students—some with disabilities, some without. All, however, have taught me much about how to instruct as well as imparted a few lessons in dedication and persistence along the way. I'd like you to meet some of these special people who have inspired me to create this book for you: Three of my students with special needs (Justin, Shery and Robert) and Sujeet Desai, a self-advocate who is at the forefront of this initiative to open the doors to music for people with special needs. His story, like the others, is inspirational and a testament to the power of music.

Sujeet Desai, 25, Down syndrome:

Sujeet Desai is an accomplished musician born with Down syndrome. Sujeet plays six instruments: Bb [B flat] and bass clarinet, alto saxophone, violin, piano and drums. In June 2001 he graduated from high school with honors and in May 2003 from the Berkshire Hills Music Academy in Massachusetts after two-year residential post-secondary study in Music and Human services. Sujeet travels around the world to do his inspirational solo performances and self-advocacy workshops.

Right after the academy graduation he started working as a teacher's aide for a music department in an elementary school. Currently he plays his music in churches, nursing homes, senior centers, hospital and various local community events as well works in a library. In July 2006 Sujeet got married to Carrie Bergeron, also a self-advocate. He lives with his wife in an apartment in Rome, New York, and enjoys his independent living.

In 1998, when Sujeet started to volunteer to provide entertainment the overwhelming response received from his audience led to his decision to make music his career. Since March 2000 he has performed in many state, national and international conferences, annual events and is booked in advance till 2008. Sujeet is a recipient of seven international awards for his music and self-advocacy.

Besides music, Sujeet has a second-degree Black Belt in martial arts (Tae Kwon Do). He has won gold and silver medals in the World Games 1999 Special Olympics in swimming and numerous medals in Special Olympics in Alpine skiing, cross-country running and bowling. He enjoys writing e-mails to his fans from all over the world who visit his Web site. Sujeet opened his Web site in 1997 in his computer graphic class, which is visited by over 107,000 people from around the world with rave reviews.

Two documentaries were done on Sujeet's life and had many television and newspaper interviews. After his trailblazing marriage to Carrie, they both were featured in *The Wall Street Journal* [and] *The New York Times*, and [had their story] aired on the national television shows "The View," "20/20," "Oprah Winfrey" and WCNY public channels.

Sindoor Desai, Sujeet's mother:

During Sujeet's nine years of school it was a continuous, frustrating struggle with school teachers to advocate for his abilities. Although I was fortunate to locate very good private teachers for each instrument, it was not easy. Sujeet has worked very hard throughout the last decade trying to become the finest musician he can be, while also working to overcome the limitations of his disability.

Music has helped him bridge this gap. With his musical versatility Sujeet has become a role model and has brought inspiration and hope to individuals with disability, their parents, educators and the services that work with them. Sujeet's family takes pride in him for all that he has brought into their lives. Currently his father and I travel with him to support him during his performances. Our mission is to send a message across the world that individuals with disabilities can, given opportunities for their abilities, "make it happen." Sujeet's music is more than just an entertainment. It's educational, inspirational and focused to make his mission possible!

Justin, 11 years old, autistic

I was told that children show their talents at a young age. My son,

Justin, was diagnosed autistic at age 3. Around this time, I made a special-occasion cake for my husband, and Justin, assuming it was his birthday, went to his toy piano and, to our surprise, started playing "Happy Birthday." A few months later, he played "Twinkle, Twinkle Little Star." He only would play with musical toys.

Through the Very Special Arts Program in New Jersey, I found a teacher who taught music to special-needs kids. At the same time we saw an ad offering pianos at a discount. We decided to make an investment in our son and bought the piano. Justin started music lessons in August 2004—with an adult music book. He plays the piano about seven times a day, from early morning to evening. My heart overflows with joy and pride when he touches the piano keys. He is my everyday miracle.

I believe music is the one universal language, which can penetrate one's heart and move people to action. Music is especially important in a special education program. It can read into the mind of the unknown and bring forth a calmer, kinder, focused child. Sadly, music is becoming an overlooked teaching tool in the school system. In an environment of cutbacks in the arts, the absence of music classes is a disservice to all, especially special-needs kids.

Justin and my daughter, who is also in the autistic spectrum, play the violin. Music, without a doubt, will nurture and mature my children into wonderful, whole human beings. It is a Godsend to have a music teacher who has the gift of song and a gift to reach children musically where many others may pass over. Music is a key to life.

—*Monica Brown, Justin's mother*

Shery Smith, 43, Down syndrome

Playing the piano is one of Shery's most cherished activities. It increases her sense of self-worth, and she quietly beams with pride at her accomplishment whenever she talks about her lessons. Just a few short years ago, she could not even use her fingers separately to form individual notes. Now, she plays with both hands, uses chords and reads music. She has progressed through at least 15 books covering show tunes, the best of John Denver, the Beatles and even some simplified classical pieces.

It's a joy for our entire family, not just because she has learned the technique of how to play the piano, but more because of what it has done for her physically, mentally and, most of all, emotionally. The fact that it is something special to her, that she can "own," was certainly clear the day she offered to have her father sit down while she accompanied him on a song he seemed to be having trouble singing! Finally, she could be in charge; she could be the helper instead of forever the one being helped. It was a wonderful moment watching her and knowing that she took another step toward realizing her own value.

—*Doris Smith, Shery's mother*

Robert Louison, 14, Down syndrome

If someone would have told me that 13 years ago when my son was born with Down syndrome, he would be able to read and play music, I probably would have doubted them. To my surprise, he can read music and play the piano. Music is a very important part in his life. He loves to listen to music and loves to perform. Music has always been prominent and important in our family, and it makes me very proud to be able to watch my son express himself through music.

—*Lynda Louison, Robert's mother*

Even though a child might be physically or mentally disabled, he should not be deprived of music. Many people think that disabled children don't have the time or the ability to concentrate on music. However, just like studies show that music helps non-disabled people with their studies and work, this is true for disabled children as well. I have evidence to prove that.

My little brother, Robert, was born with Down syndrome. This results in a mental and physical disability including low muscle tone. However, with the help of Robert's occupational therapist, Karen, he is able to take weekly lessons practicing the piano. Fortunately for us, Karen has worked with many students with disabilities and has also taken on her passion of piano playing on the side. This enables her to provide the best learning experience for my brother. He is very comfortable with her as well, since she is his favorite teacher.

Robert takes one piano lesson a week for about an hour. They work on the names of the notes and where you place your fingers. Just recently, he's been progressing more than ever. He has performed in a couple of recitals with Karen's other students.

We always talk about how it would be if Robert wasn't disabled, and how he would be yet another member of the Louison family passing through the band program at Randolph High School, giving my mother four more years of high school band. However, he has shown us that he has the music gene and is very passionate about it. This proves that children with disabilities can have the opportunity to learn music just like the rest of us.

—Michael Louison, Robert's brother

Sally Tucker, teacher

Several years ago I attended the Piano Teachers Camp at Westminster Choir College in Princeton, New Jersey. I had recently left my job of 14 years in the pharmaceutical industry to pursue a career in music. I had not started teaching prior to attending the camp. I was just feeling the waters to see if teaching was for me. One of the lectures that particularly caught my interest was given by Karen Kowalski, who spoke about special students and mentioned there was a shortage of piano teachers willing to take on these individuals. Her lecture made such an impact on me. I approached Karen after her lecture and said that I was very interested in learning more about teaching students with special needs. A few weeks later, I received an e-mail from her asking if I would be interested in teaching a student with Asperger's Syndrome. At first I thought, "Geez, I haven't had any experience teaching normal kids. How am I going to be able to teach a kid with special needs?" However, I responded: "Yes, I'd love to!"

I am so glad I did. Words cannot describe how rewarding it is it to work with special-needs students. After several years, I have discovered that teaching a student with special needs is not much different than teaching the mainstream child. Each child, regardless of label/ability, has his own special needs. For example, one might have difficulty keeping a beat, but can sight-read amazingly well, while another may be able to keep a beat, but has difficulty sight-reading. Hence, I adjust the curriculum accordingly. It is similar to teaching a child with special needs.

Prior to teaching this type of child, I thought I would have to simplify my methods. I couldn't have been more wrong. Perhaps it was the luck of the draw, but the special-needs kids who have come to me for lessons have been extremely high-functioning. Many have been able to sight-read better than my "mainstream" students. Their sensitivity to sound enables them to phrase impeccably. Some have an amazing ability to memorize. One student, a 6-year-old boy with autism, started lessons with me two months ago as a beginner and already has memorized the first two volumes of the Faber & Faber "In Recital" books. He also can play one of the three-page pieces from memory backward with perfect phrasing. This student is one of my most dedicated. He insists on playing all of the pieces he has learned in sequential order prior to leaving for school each morning. How many of your mainstreamed students practice that diligently?

Please consider taking on students with special needs, particularly if you enjoy a challenge. It does take a lot of patience and intuition. Be sensitive to all students. Find out what makes them tick. Make each child feel special, regardless of ability or label. If the child wants to learn, then he will. Respect the child, and the child will respect you. Use lots of positive reinforcement. Play for your students often, even when they appear not to be listening. You would be surprised at the amount of information they absorb. Most importantly, convey your love of music and teaching. The rewards are endless.

Afterword

Now we come to the part of the book where you take off your training wheels and go. It will be a learning process for you as well as your student. Eventually it will become easier and you, too, will develop your own "tricks" to teaching as I did. At this point, you should have a beginning understanding about the differences between the students both with and without special needs. More importantly, you should know their similarities—both have the ability and desire to learn music.

I would like to thank the many people who helped make this book a reality through their efforts, talents, inspiration and support: Patti Verbanas (my sister and editor); Leeza Hernandez (illustrator and designer); Ed Pagliarini (photographer); Mary Afiouni, Doris and Phil Smith, Lynda Louison, Monica Brown, Sindoor Desai and Anabela Rossi (parents of special-needs musicians); Sally Tucker (contributor); Chris Mansolino (Web designer); Sr. Helene Marie, Sr. Delores Margaret, Dr. Hoyle, Carmella Thompson, John Harrity and Tom Brislin (my music teachers past and present); the staff at the P.G. Chambers School and Somerville School of Music; Edward and Ann Zielinski (my parents) and Kevin Zielinski (my brother), as well as my dearest husband, Stephen, for his encouragement and frank honesty. Finally, I would like to thank all of my piano students past and present for being my greatest teachers and inspiration, most notably: Summer, Shery, Nikki, Robert, Justin and Serena.

Hopefully this book has inspired you to take that first step: Answer the phone and agree to teach one individual with special needs. It could be the most life-altering thing you do.

About the Author

Karen Z. Kowalski is a pediatric occupational therapist at the P.G. Chambers School in Cedar Knolls, New Jersey, and is a classically trained pianist who began learning music at age 5. Since 1995, she has taught piano to students with and without special needs (cerebral palsy, autism, developmental delays and Down syndrome) at the Somerville School of Music in New Jersey, where she developed the institution's music program for individuals with special needs. For the past six years she has directed an adaptive bell choir program at the P.G. Chambers School for children with special needs.

Kowalski has published articles on her innovative approach of combining occupational therapy with music theory in *Exceptional Parent Magazine, Journal for the Association of Schools and Agencies for the Handicapped* and *Advance for Occupational Therapy Practitioners.* She has lectured on her approach at the Westminster Choir College in Princeton, New Jersey.

Kowalski received a B.S. in Occupational Therapy along with a music minor from Kean University in Union, New Jersey, and a Master of Public Health degree from the University of Medicine and Dentistry in Piscataway, New Jersey.

Resources

ASSOCIATIONS

American Academy of Pediatrics.
>   (847) 434-4000. www.aap.org.

Autism Society of America.
>   (800) 328-8476. www.autism-society.org.

Children and Adults with Attention Deficit/Hyperactivity Disorder.
>   (800) 233-4050. www.chadd.org.

Learning Disabilities Association of America.
>   (412) 341-1515. www.ldaamerica.org.

National Down Syndrome Society.
>   (800) 221-4602. www.ndss.org.

Sensory Integration International.
>   (310) 787-8805. www.sensoryint.com.

The National Association for Music Education.
>   (800) 336-3768. www.menc.org.

Tourette Syndrome Association.
>   (718) 224-2999. www.tsa-usa.org.

United Cerebral Palsy.
>   (800) 872-5827. www.ucp.org.

References

Children with Cerebral Palsy: A Parent's Guide, Elaine Geralis, ed. (Woodbine House Inc., 1998).

Color By Interval series (books 1 and 2) by Sharon Kaplan (Alfred Publishing).

Color By Note series (books 1 and 2) by Sharon Kaplan (Alfred Publishing).

Color By Note Monsters by Sharon Kaplan (Alfred Publishing).

Complete Learning Disabilities Handbook: Ready-To-Use Strategies & Activities for Teaching Students with Learning Disabilities, New Second Edition by Joan M. Harwell (Jossey-Bass, 2001).

Diagnostic and Statistical Manual of Mental Disorders-Fourth Edition (DSM-IV) (American Psychiatric Association, Washington D.C., 1994).

Fine Motor Skills for Children with Down Syndrome: A Guide for Parents and Professionals (Topics in Down Syndrome), second edition, by Maryanne Bruni (Woodbine House, 2006).

Gross Motor Skills in Children with Down Syndrome: A Guide for Parents and Professionals by Patricia C. Winders (Woodbine House, 1997).

Sensory Integration and the Child by A. Jean Ayres (Western Psychological Services, 1979).

The Out of Sync Child: Recognizing and Coping With Sensory Integration Dysfunction, by Carol Stock Kranowitz (Perigee Books, 1998).

Theory for Young Musicians-Notespeller, music by Carla Ulbrich (Alfred Publishing, 2006).

Thinking in Pictures: and Other Reports from My Life with Autism by Temple Grandin (DoubleDay Dell Publishing Group, 1995).

Tics and Tourette Syndrome: A Handbook for Parents and Professionals by Uttom Chowdhury, Isobel Heyman (foreword) (Jessica Kingsley Publishers, 2004).

When the Brain Can't Hear: Unraveling the Mystery of Auditory Processing Disorder by Teri James Bellis, Ph.D. (Atria, reprint edition, 2003).

Contact

MOUSEBOX BOOKS
www.mouseboxbooks.com

m b b

Contact:
karen@mouseboxbooks.com

Or call toll-free:
(866) 668 - 7055

Mailing Address:
116 West Cliff Street, Somerville, NJ 08876

Notes

Notes

Printed in the USA
CPSIA information can be obtained
at www.ICGtesting.com
LVHW011631210824
788893LV00031B/365